ELC

RIVERSIDE PUBLIC LIBRARY

P9-CJO-935

WAUCONDA PUBLIC LIBRARY

Native American Life

Plank Houses

by Karen Bush Gibson

Consultant:
Troy Rollen Johnson, PhD
American Indian Studies
California State University
Long Beach, California

Capstone
press

Mankato, Minnesota

Bridgestone Books are published by Capstone Press,
151 Good Counsel Drive, P.O. Box 669, Mankato, Minnesota 56002.
www.capstonepress.com

Copyright © 2005 by Capstone Press. All rights reserved.
No part of this publication may be reproduced in whole or in part, or stored in a retrieval
system, or transmitted in any form or by any means, electronic, mechanical, photocopying,
recording, or otherwise, without written permission of the publisher.
For information regarding permission, write to Capstone Press,
151 Good Counsel Drive, P.O. Box 669, Dept. R, Mankato, Minnesota 56002.
Printed in the United States of America

Library of Congress Cataloging-in-Publication Data
Gibson, Karen Bush.
Plank houses / by Karen Bush Gibson.
    p. cm.—(Bridgestone books. Native American life)
    Includes bibliographical references and index.
    ISBN 0-7368-3725-6 (hardcover)
    1. Indians of North America—Dwellings. I. Title. II. Series: Bridgestone Books:
Native American life (Mankato, Minn.)
E98.D9G53 2005
728'.089'97—dc22
                                                      2004011215

Summary: A brief introduction to plank houses, including the materials, construction, and people who
    lived in these traditional Native American dwellings.

Editorial Credits
Roberta Basel and Katy Kudela, editors; Jennifer Bergstrom, designer; Jo Miller, photo researcher;
    Scott Thoms, photo editor

Photo Credits
Art Resource, NY/Werner Forman, 8 (inset); Bruce Coleman Inc./E&P Bauer, 8; Corbis/Danny
Lehman, cover; Corbis/Gunter Marx Photography, 1, 4; Corbis/Joel W. Rogers, 10; Corbis/Stuart
Westmorland, 20; Illustration by Gordon Miller, 16; Marilyn "Angel" Wynn, 18; The University of
Michigan Exhibit Museum (Photo altered with permission), 6; University of Washington Libraries,
Special Collections, NA3854, 12; University of Washington Libraries, Special Collections, NA2547, 14

1 2 3 4 5 6 10 09 08 07 06 05

Table of Contents

4

What Is a Plank House?

Plank houses are made of wide boards called planks. These houses had one door in the front. They did not have any windows. Many plank houses had a **totem pole** above the doorway.

Plank houses looked like large square or rectangular boxes. Smaller plank houses were 40 to 60 feet (12 to 18 meters) long. Larger homes were about 100 feet (30 meters) long.

◄ A totem pole often marked the entrance to a plank house.

Who Lived in a Plank House?

Native Americans of the Northwest Coast once lived in plank houses. They lived near the Pacific Ocean from southern Alaska to northern California. These **tribes** included the Chinook, Haida, and Tlingit.

Many related families lived together in a plank house. Families included aunts, uncles, cousins, and grandparents.

Today, Native American tribes still use a few of these **traditional** homes. They build and use plank houses for community centers.

◀ Northwest Coast tribes lived along the Pacific Ocean.

Gathering Materials

Native Americans gathered wood from nearby forests to build plank houses. They used tools made of stone and bone to chop down trees. The wood was made into **beams**, posts, poles, and planks.

Many tribes used cedar trees. A cedar tree can grow up to 230 feet (70 meters) high. Such a large tree could provide enough wood for one entire plank house. The cedar tree would even provide wood to build canoes and totem poles.

◄ Builders used stone tools (inset) to cut the cedar trees.

Preparing the Materials

Preparing the wood for a plank house took many steps. After cutting down a tree, people cut off the branches. They then removed the bark. They used the bark to make rope.

Builders used most of the tree to make planks. They pounded **wedges** into the tree with a stone hammer. The wedges split the wood into long, thin planks.

◀ A large cedar tree could give a builder enough wood to make planks for an entire plank house.

Building a Plank House

Building a plank house began with the **frame**. The builders dug holes and set heavy posts in the ground. They used ropes to lift beams onto the posts. They then built the frame of the roof with thinner poles.

Builders used wood planks to finish the walls and roof of the house. They joined the planks to the frame with wood pegs. They also used narrow strips of bark or cloth.

Builders often carved a totem pole. The figures on the pole stood for the **ancestors** of the families who lived in the plank house.

◄ Tlingit men carve designs into a totem pole. Each tribe had its own totem pole design.

Inside a Plank House

Most plank houses had an area for cooking. Everyone in the house shared this space. The cooking area was dug into the ground. Fires were lit in this pit. The house's plank floor was built higher than the fire pit.

Each family had its own space along the walls of the house. Screens or boxes separated them. A family area included a wide bench. People covered the benches with mats and furs. They slept and sat on the benches.

◀ People shared a cooking space in the center of the plank house.

Plank House Villages

Native Americans of the Northwest Coast built their plank houses in rows. Small villages had one row of plank houses. Larger villages had several rows of plank houses.

Tribes often built their villages near the ocean or a river. They built canoes to travel on the water. People caught salmon and shellfish to eat.

◀ Tribes set up villages near the ocean or by rivers. The plank houses always faced the water.

Special Plank Houses

Each village had special plank houses. Some buildings were used for **ceremonies**. People gathered in these buildings to act out stories with masks.

Some villages also had special plank houses called sweat houses. People built this house over a fire pit filled with rocks. They poured water on the hot rocks to make steam. The low ceiling of the sweat house kept the steam inside. The village men would visit the sweat house. It was a place for teaching, storytelling, and singing.

◄ A sweat house had a low roof to keep the steam inside.

Totem Poles

Many Northwest Coast tribes decorated their plank houses. People painted animals, birds, and people on their houses. Some people built totem poles. Builders carved totem poles out of red cedar trees. Each animal and human form carved into the totem poles had a story.

Today, Northwest Coast Indians still carve totem poles. Totem poles have become one of the most well-known cultural items of the Northwest Coast Indians.

◄ Colorful totem poles are a part of many plank houses.

Glossary

ancestor (AN-sess-tur)—a family member who lived long ago

beam (BEEM)—a long, thick piece of wood used to support the roof of a plank house

ceremony (SER-uh-moh-nee)—formal actions, words, and often music performed to mark an important occasion

frame (FRAYM)—the basic shape over which a house is built

totem pole (TOH-tuhm POHL)—a pole carved and painted with animals and other objects that represent a family

traditional (truh-DISH-uhn-uhl)—using the styles, manners, and ways of the past

tribe (TRIBE)—a group of people who share the same ancestors, customs, and laws

wedge (WEJ)—an object that has a wide end and a narrow end; wedges are used to cut or split apart objects.

Read More

Dyer, Dolores A. *Plank House.* Native American Homes. Vero Beach, Fla.: Rourke, 2001.

Kalman, Bobbie. *Native Homes.* Native Nations of North America. New York: Crabtree, 2001.

Internet Sites

FactHound offers a safe, fun way to find Internet sites related to this book. All of the sites on FactHound have been researched by our staff.

Here's how:
1. Visit *www.facthound.com*
2. Type in this special code **0736837256** for age-appropriate sites. Or enter a search word related to this book for a more general search.
3. Click on the **Fetch It** button.

FactHound will fetch the best sites for you!

Index